D0618981

Painting
the
Fence

by Geoff Patton
illustrated by David Clarke

RISING★STARS

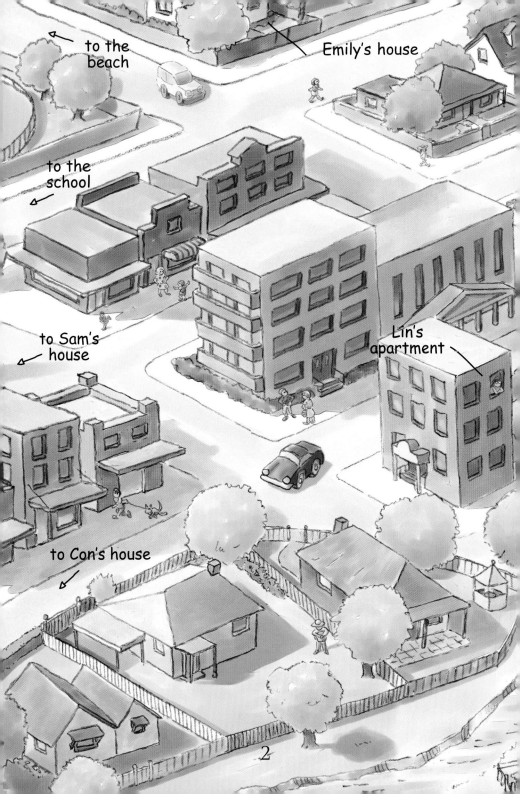

Mrs Mac's
farm

Toola
Oola

Emily
Rimmerly

4

Hi. My name is Lin.

These are my friends.

Chapter 1
The Fence

Mum says, 'Today is the day for painting the fence.'
I say, 'I just *love* to paint. Can I paint the fence?'

'Yes,' says Mum. 'You can paint the fence.'

I paint and paint, but it is a very
long fence. There is only one of me.
I will never get it done!

'Maybe I don't *love* painting
after all,' I say to myself.

And then along comes Jenna Yoon.

Chapter 2
Jenna Lends a Hand

'Hi, Jenna Yoon,' I say. 'I am painting the fence and it's *so* much fun.'
Jenna Yoon says, 'I just *love* to paint. Can I paint too?'

I just *love* to paint.

I say, 'Jenna Yoon, because you are such a good friend, you can help me paint. All you need is some paint and a brush.'

Soon Jenna Yoon comes back with a
brush and some very yellow paint.

We paint and paint, but it is a very
long fence. There are only two of us.
We will never get it done!

'Maybe I don't *love* painting after all,' says Jenna Yoon.

And then along
comes Veronica Pickles.

Chapter 3
Veronica to the Rescue

'Hi, Veronica Pickles,' we say. 'We are painting the fence and it's so much fun.' Veronica Pickles says, 'I just *love* to paint. Can I paint too?'

I just *love* to paint.

We say, 'Veronica Pickles, because you are such a good friend, you can help us paint.'
'All you need is some paint and a brush,' says Jenna Yoon.

Soon Veronica Pickles comes
back with a brush and some
very purple paint.

We paint and paint, but it is
a very long fence. There are
only three of us.
Will we ever get it done?

'Maybe I don't *love* painting after all,'
says Veronica Pickles.

And then along
comes Emily Rimmerly.

Chapter 4
Can Emily Paint?

'Hi, Emily Rimmerly,' we all say. 'We are painting the fence and it's so much fun.' Emily Rimmerly says, 'I just *love* to paint. Can I paint too?'

I just *love* to paint.

We say, 'Emily Rimmerly, because you are such a good friend, you can help us paint.'
'All you need is paint and a brush,' says Veronica Pickles.

Soon Emily Rimmerly
comes back with a brush
and some very red paint.

We paint and paint, but it is
a very long fence. There are
only four of us.
Will we ever get it done?

'Maybe I don't *love* painting after all,' says Emily Rimmerly.

And then along comes Toola Oola.

Chapter 5
Help Toola!

'Hi, Toola Oola,' we all say. 'We are painting the fence and it's so much fun.' Toola Oola says, 'I just *love* to paint. Can I paint too?'

I just *love* to paint.

We say, 'Toola Oola, because you are such a good friend, you can help us paint.'
'All you need is paint and a brush,' says Emily Rimmerly.

Soon Toola Oola comes back with
a brush and some very orange
paint. We paint and paint, but it's
a very long fence. There are only
five of us.

Will we ever get it done?
And then along comes Mum.

'Hi,' we all say. 'We are painting
the fence and it's so much fun.'
Mum says, 'I just love to paint.
Too bad it's all finished!'

'Finished!' says Toola Oola.
'Finished!' says Emily Rimmerly.
'Finished!' says Veronica Pickles.
'Finished!' says Jenna Yoon.
'Finished!' I say.

'Just when we were having
so much fun!'

Survival Tips

1 Tell your friends that you are having a party. When they get there, hand them a paint brush.

2 Make the paint runny. Runny paint goes on much easier.

3 Save up your homework to do on fence-painting day.

4 Use a big brush.
You get more done
that way.

5 Eat plenty of
chocolate. Painting
needs lots of energy.

6 Remember that you
have to visit Gran,
who lives on the
other side of town!

Riddles and Jokes

Emily Veronica, Veronica, I feel like an apple!

Veronica Don't worry, I won't bite.

Toola Lin, Lin, I have ringing in my ears!

Lin Well answer it!

Veronica If I had five paint brushes in one hand and six in the other, what would I have?

Lin Very big hands.

Jenna Knock, knock.

Emily Who's there?

Jenna Water.

Emily Water who?

Jenna Water friends for?